The Bloom After Rain

Where Sorrow Ends, A New Love Begins

The Bloom After Rain

Where Sorrow Ends, A New Love Begins

Dr. Sougat Dasgupta

Anecdote
Publishing House
For the love of quality reading!

Anecdote
Publishing House
For the love of quality reading!

anecdotepublishinghouse.com
champreaders.com

Anecdote Publishing House
2nd Floor 2/15 Lane no. 2 Ansari Road, Daryaganj-110002
Email: info@anecdotepublishinghouse.com
Website: anecdotepublishinghouse.com

Published by Anecdote Publishing House

First Edition 2025
ISBN 978-81-982589-4-6
MRP ₹ 350

Book Promoted and Marketed by Champ Readers Pvt. Ltd.
Editorial Process: Meraki
Cover design by: Rishikumar Thakur
Layout by: Arivazhagi Balasundaram
Printed in India

Note From the Poet

This book is, in many ways, the echo of a long conversation I've had with myself—sometimes in silence, sometimes in storm. *The Bloom After Rain* is not merely a collection of poems. It is a map of my emotional landscape, traced from the tremors of adolescence to the layered quietude of adulthood. If you listen closely, you might hear the voice of a boy learning the language of longing—and the man he eventually became, still speaking it.

Though much of my life is devoted to the mystical geometry of astrology, these poems are carved from a more intimate space—my inner seasons, the shifting weather of love, loss, memory, and becoming. They are pieces of me that lived hidden for years, and finally found their voice on paper.

My literary bloodline runs through Tennyson, T.S. Eliot, and Rabindranath Tagore. I grew old reading them. I learned English feeling the weight of their words. Their rhythms are ghosted in these pages—sometimes grand, sometimes aching, always honest. And yes, you might catch a whiff of old Bollywood melodies lingering in some verses, like forgotten cassettes playing on a monsoon afternoon.

I'm unapologetically old school. I believe nostalgia is a kind of truth too.

More than anything, this is *my voice*—raw, unmasked, and real. The love I could not say out loud. The grief I carried like folded letters. The moments I couldn't share with anyone but the page.

I hope that somewhere in these poems, you find yourself again. Perhaps in the ache of first love. Or in the healing that comes, slowly, faithfully, like rain.

And if you do—may you, too, bloom after it.

Keep reading.
Keep blooming.

With love and light,

Acknowledgments

With reverence that words can scarcely hold, I offer my deepest gratitude to every soul who, knowingly or quietly, walked beside me on the long and luminous journey that birthed *The Bloom After Rain.* This collection is not merely a gathering of poems—it is the trace of a becoming, the afterglow of heartbreaks endured, silences listened to, and the quiet triumph of blooming through shadows.

At the sacred centre of this journey stands Dr.Surajit Sen—my mentor, my guiding constellation. His magnum opus, *The Maiden Flight,* did more than inspire; it awakened something ancestral within me. His command over language, his lyrical austerity, his fearless pursuit of inner truth—these became the first winds that lifted my own faltering flight. I write today not in imitation, but in continuation of the language he once placed in my hands like fire—alive, demanding, and holy.

To my parents, who have been both root and roof—your faith was never loud, but always present. In the quiet of your blessings, this bloom found its earth.

To my devoted team, thank you for being the unspoken architecture beneath each poem—for believing, even when the ink had not yet dried, that something sacred was forming. Your silence was not absence—it was trust, and I felt it.

And to Ankita Shil, my manager, and quiet guardian of this vision—your meticulous presence, your patient vigilance, and the gentleness with which you tended to each fragile line, ensured this book was not just completed, but cared for. You preserved its soul.

This book breathes because of all of you.

My pen was mine, but the wind was yours.

With all my heart,

Dedicated to

Someone Very Special,
For whom, "I BLOOMED AFTER THE RAIN"

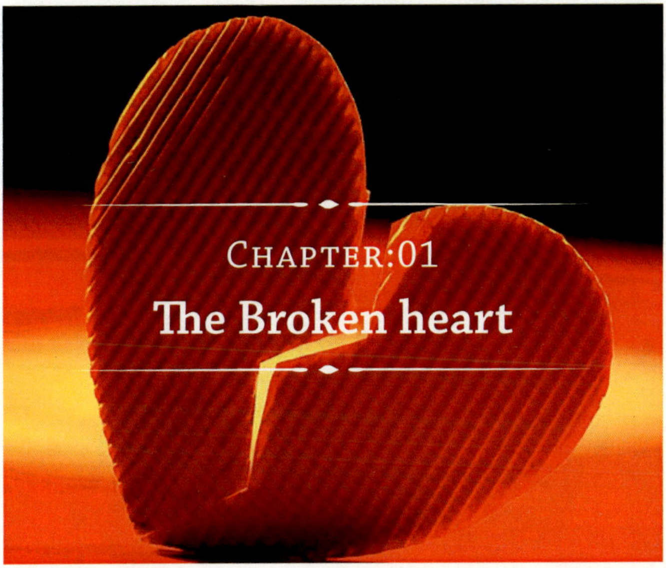

CHAPTER:01

The Broken heart

An Incomplete Love

You came closer to me,
Yet still, there was distance.
I fell in love with you,
As sleep falls to a fatigued organ.
Perhaps the sky never needed the land,
As I needed you
Perhaps the moonlight was never as tender
As you were to me.
I longed to speak, to hold your hand again
But it was a love that was never meant to begin.
I seemed to have collided with your fragrance,
Which made me forget all my penance.
I began to weave a "necklace of poems" for you,
Which you took as a gift,
And in return, you offered me
That age-old pain,
Which my spellbound heart gracefully received.
I even forgot the way back,
As we walked together,
And now, you have left me here,
Writing something like my name

In the sands of your love.
Our incomplete love shall never begin,
And you became an image,
To be remembered, again and again.

Why Is Love a Sin?

Something was broken, yet never fell;
The silence of my soul deepened instead,
Sinking into its solitary well,
Brooding unseen among the dead.
My love for her was an autumnal tide,
A river, full and fierce and free;
My verses murmured like a woodland stream,
That once brought her delight and ease.
Yet in a single fleeting hour, all turned
And I was left to bear the blame.
O life, permit me yet to breathe;
Do not bind me forever to shame.
I fell with her into infinite dreams,
And shaped our future in golden skies;
O tell me, life, with all your storms
Why must love be called a crime?
I worshipped her through reverent eyes,
And felt her spirit bound to mine;
As if, beyond the veils of time,
Our souls had known love's ancient sign.
I loved her laughter's innocent grace,
And poured my being at her feet;

Tell me, life, if love was pure,
Why did you doom me to defeat?
Why cast me down to the broken vale?
Why drown my dreams in nameless pain?
Answer me, life
Why is love a sin?

A Song Half Sung

You sang to me beneath the twilight boughs,
a canticle that brushed the breath of stars.
It stirred the velvet silence of the glade,
and shimmered through the dusk like silver spars.
Your voice became the pulse within my chest,
a woven spell that stilled the winds of doubt.
I built my life on every trembling chord—
a temple raised from praise the soul poured out.
But mid-refrain, you turned your gaze aside,
and let the fragile cadence come undone.
Now echoes haunt the hollow of that verse,
where once the warmth of morning light had shone.
The notes you left still ache within my bones,
each one a revenant I cannot flee.
The stillness nestled 'tween your vanished words
now thunders louder than your melody.
No final strain, no closing bow was drawn
you lost the song and vanished into night.
And I must bear the silence left aloft,
still hanging like a wound in failing light.
A song half sung becomes a sacred scar—
no voice can close; no time can tune or bar.

The Rain Remembers

The rain returns on April's grieving breath,
and graces earth with steps too soft to hear.
It taps the pane like hands that once were yours,
recalling vows the wind refused to clear.
I walk beneath a sky of weeping glass,
where once your fingers laced themselves with mine.
Though dusk has drawn its veil across the fields,
the air still stirs with remnants of our time.
You spoke of love as petals speak of spring
with fleeting grace, with fragrance bound to fade.
Yet now the clouds repeat your vanished voice,
and echo back the promises you made.
I called your name into the hungering dusk,
but only silence echoed from the trees.
The rain replied in elegies of dusk,
in drops that wrote your absence on my knees.
Still do I roam the silver-laden paths,
where once your laughter mingled into mine.
I've learned what longing teaches through the years
that love may go, but ache remains divine.
For rain recalls what wayward hearts conceal,
and mourns the loss you taught me how to feel.

The Curtain Drawn Too Late

I stood upon the stage we shared,
reciting lines you once believed.
But you had gone behind the veil—
and I, alone, was left deceived.
Your part was played with gentle art,
your eyes still held the proper light.
But in your voice, a hollow rang—
and love was fading out of sight.
The curtain rose, the house was full,
yet not a soul could see the truth.
I bowed, I smiled, I spoke of dreams—
while bleeding quiet from my youth.
You sought another script to read,
another cast, another play.
While I remained where vows were made,
still tethered to our yesterday.
Now silence sits upon the boards,
where once your laughter knew its place.
The echoes stir, then fall apart,
like light withdrawn from time and space.
And though the final act has passed,
I still await your shadowed trace.

Ruin by Whisper

Not by thunder did you break me,
nor storm, nor wrath, nor sharpened tongue.
But by a whisper faintly spun,
a secret low, so softly sung.
A single thread, a careless name,
let loose behind the door at dusk
it found my ear, it found my trust,
and turned our bed to ash and dust.
You smiled the same, and kissed my brow,
and tucked your lies beneath the sheets.
But truth, once loosed, will not be caged
it crawls through cracks; it will not sleep.
I watched it bloom like mold on silk,
the beauty spoiled from deep within.
And all we built with sacred hands
was razed by what you kept akin.
You wounded not by hand or word,
but by the things you did not tell.
And now, amid this shattered calm,
I walk through love's extinguished shell.
A whisper held can weigh like stone
and silence rings where trust has flown.

Remains of the Hour

There was a minute before the lie,
a slender breath between the truths,
where love sat still upon the sill
and time forgot to move its tooth.
You passed me tea in porcelain calm
your fingers did not tremble then.
But the cup was cracked beneath its glaze,
and I drank it all, again and again.
You had already gone, I see it now,
though your shadow lingered in the room.
The clock did not tick that final day
it sighed, and settled into gloom.
There was no thunder in your leaving,
no grand betrayal, no shattered glass.
Just quiet omissions, carefully placed,
and time, like ash, began to pass.
I now collect these silent grains
a name unsaid, a glance askew.
The hour remains, the body fades,
but something false still flickers through.
And in the stillness, I remain
part grief, part ghost, part rue.

The Echo of Your Parting

You left, and still the days move on,
with sunlit masks and measured pace.
Yet time, though robed in golden light,
has not the power to erase.
I smiled beneath the morning wind,
as if my grief were but a mist.
But silence bloomed where words once grew
and joy withdrew its final kiss.
You vanished like the trailing mist
that lifts before the dawn can bloom.
And still I find your shadow pressed
against each corner of the room.
No storm declared your swift retreat,
no closing door, no parting cry.
Only a pause where once was breath,
and then the long, unanswered sky.
I wander through the hours' wreck,
through tea grown cold and letters torn.
Love, once a throne of living gold,
now lies in shreds, forgotten, worn.
You left with grace, as cowards do
and grace is oft the keenest wound.

The Broken One's Question

Someone once asked me,
"How often does she visit your thought?"
I smiled through the silence and said,
"As many times as my eyelids close and open
As many times as breath forgets to be sought."
He asked again,
Then he leaned closer and asked,
"How deeply do you love her?"
I replied,
"As countless as the stars scattered across heaven's endless dome."
"Why does her memory cling so?"
And I murmured,
"Because I have loved her in myriad forms,
And shall love her still,
Flowing through her memory as rivers surrender to the sea.
My love for her is no less than life itself
It is my beginning, my end, my eternity."
He smiled, a little broken smile, and whispered,
"Tell me, does she love you the same?"
Ah, dear heart

I had no answer to proclaim.
You dwelled near my soul,
As the pasture clings to the patient earth;
But was I ever near to you, O dear?
This question, like a lonely bird, still flies unheard.
And who was he, who asked me thus?
None but the broken one
None but myself.

The Question That Remains

Why did you tread upon my quiet shore,
Only to vanish, leaving me no more?
Why did you awaken love's restless sigh,
If all you meant was to let it die?
Why weave your soul into mine so deep,
If you had only promises to break, not keep?
By your gentle touch, my heart learned to sing;
By you alone, it learned the pain of losing everything.
In the shadowed corners of my silent eyes,
Tears slept — you taught them to rise.
O beloved, answer me this
Why did you come,
Only to leave me lost in the abyss?
When my gaze found yours, trembling and shy,
Strange embers rose, unbidden, to the sky.
Why did you teach my heart to soar so high,
Only to let it fall, and forget to ask why?

How can I forget?

How can I ever relinquish that vision,
The first time your image graced my sight?
A presence so pure, so transcendent,
Like dawn's first light, breaking the night.
How can I erase that hallowed moment,
When your voice, like a whispering breeze,
Caressed my ear, a sweet, tender sermon,
Filling my heart with an endless ease?
I stood at the shore, with waves at my feet,
Yet your voice, like music, claimed the air
A melody that matched the ocean's heartbeat,
Resonating in stillness, calm and rare.
The world dissolved, became a shadowed veil,
As your love, like the sea, reached my soul
How could I forget, how could I fail,
To remember when your voice made me whole?
O radiant muse, whose image still gleams,
Are you but a dream woven from the sea?
If this be illusion, I dare not awaken,
For in this reverie, your love is all I see.

Let me remain suspended in this trance,
Where time ceases in your gaze so bright,
In your love, I seek no waking chance,
But only to linger within this endless night.

A Silent Pain

I have known your presence across a thousand nameless dawns,
As I sit alone, adrift upon the sea of thought, yearning to hear
Your nightingale voice, tremulous with unspoken fear.
Still, in the silence, I hear your forgotten songs for me
And feel the tender ache, the shy sweetness of every stolen meeting,
Where our hearts, untamed, would hasten in secret beating.
When I cast my mind adrift upon the shores of our youth,
Countless memories rise like sacred incense to the skies,
And my soul replays those hallowed hours
My heart, in all its weathers, could never deny.
Each time I remember you,
I taste the wistful sorrow that shadows love's beauty;
Each time your name brushes against my ear,
I am wounded anew by that silent, aching tear.
Through the vast corridors of language,

I seek in vain the word that might hold
The measure of my love for you
A love that speaks not, yet floods the soul.
In the brief concourse of your passing nearness,
My world is kindled anew in strange, wondrous light;
Yet I have lost myself to a faltering dream
A sorrowful exile,
A wound from which no solace will ever stream.

The Silence After You

I laid my soul within your care,
as rivers yield to the quiet sea;
I spoke your name in breath and prayer,
and stitched it through the life in me.
You were the keeper of my light,
the dream I held with trembling hands;
but you turned away to other skies,
and left our bond like broken strands.
The home we built with softest sighs,
now falters in its frail decline;
its walls are dust, its hearth grown cold
and I, alone, walk through its shrine.
I do not curse; I do not call;
my tears have learned to fall in grace.
There is a silence after love
a hush no voice can now replace.
You were the song I tried to keep;
you were the flame I could not save.
Now sorrow walks beside my steps
and names me faithful to the grave.

A Farewell Beneath Silent Skies

The memories of our love
lie strewn like petals upon the winds of my heart.
Once I believed
no sorrow could unravel the thread that bound our souls.
I laboured to keep the flame aglow,
to cradle our bond in hands of hope;
but destiny, inscrutable and austere,
parted us, as silent storms part the seas.
Oft my spirit strays to those tender hours,
when side by side we sat,
speaking in the eloquence of glances.
I know
somewhere within you too—the echoes remain:
the smile that once lit your face,
now reawakens the ache of longing in my own.
I gather those lost days
like scattered blooms pressed to a grieving heart,
and in their fragrance,
I murmur a last, aching farewell.
The day you turned away,
a silence vaster than sorrow enveloped me.

I stood alone,
wrapped in the bewilderment of a world made strange.
A portion of my very being was severed,
yet no path led me toward its recovery
it was as though the book of our lives
had been left forever unfinished;
for in losing you,
I had lost the finest friend my heart had ever known.
Still, I send my prayers to the silent heavens,
that light may fall upon your path,
that your dreams may gather wings
and you may rise, unfettered,
into the boundless fields of joy.
O, would that this were but a fleeting dream!
For I miss you beyond the reach of words
Yet you are summoned by your destiny to soar.
And thus, with trembling hands,
and a soul heavy with benedictions,
I offer you my last,
most tender goodbye.

When Trust Became a Stranger

I placed my soul like a prayer in your hands,
and watched it vanish into winds I could not name.
I wrote your name upon my morning skies,
and sowed your dreams in the fields of my heart.
You, in whose light my spirit once bloomed,
turned your eyes to distant, hungering shores.
You traded the garden we had nurtured in silence
for the fleeting fragrance of another's breath.
The house of song we built with tender sighs
crumbles now into dust between my palms.
Its pillars of hope collapse in the hush of twilight,
and I walk its ruins with unshod feet.
I lift no hand to summon your shadow,
nor weep to the heavens for your return.
Only the hollow ache of forsaken trust
beats like a broken drum within my chest.
I offer no malice, no bitter lament;
I fold my sorrow like linen in the dark.
I bear my wound with the silence of stars,
and walk on, crowned by the ruin of love.

Whisper of the Vanished One

She fled as mist before the pitiless morn,
No token left, no sigh, no parting sworn;
Her shadow melted through the trembling air,
Leaving the skies in a hollowed, wordless prayer.
Was she but dream — a blossom of the skies?
Or mortal song that time itself denies?
Her laughter once had lit the sleeping rose,
Now only in grief silent gardens grows.
I called her name — no echo gave reply,
The winds wept on, the river wandered by;
Her touch, once soft as twilight on the seas,
Now fades like incense on a dying breeze.
Her absence carves its thorns across my sleep,
A sorrow vast, a yearning dark and deep;
Yet in the ruin where her silence clings,
A broken fragrance stirs forgotten wings.
Was she my fate — or a phantom guest,
Who kissed my soul and vanished with the rest?

The Name That Haunts Me Still

Your name arrived—not spoken—breathed,
a relic drifting through the dusk,
neither prayer nor invocation,
but a residue of trust.
The lamps were lit. The tea was cold.
The books remained half-read, half-known.
The shadows stretched along the wall
and made the silence not my own.
You left, or rather... faded out
no final word, no sharp goodbye.
A door was closed behind a thought,
and thought itself refused to die.
Time wears a face I do not know
its hands are thin; its lips are dry.
It counts the things we left unsaid
and trades the truth for alibi.
I do not beg you to return,
nor grieve the warmth in stranger arms
I grieve the self I once became,
when held within your fleeting charms.
Your name is not a name, but weight
it rings in me like broken glass,

a bell struck once and left to hum
in corridors where echoes pass.
And still it hums. And still, I wait
though not for you, but what you were.
Some names outlive the ones they named,
and haunt the air like ancient stir.

The Gift of Your Forgetfulness

Thanks, O thanks to you,
for the gift of sorrow, you left upon my soul.
It was my folly, mine alone,
to lay my heart, trembling, in your careless hands.
The love you offered bore no flame,
no warmth to shelter my seeking spirit.
Yet I raise no voice against you,
for the fault was mine, and mine alone.
Thanks, O thanks to you,
for the burden of grief you placed in my hands.
In the silent watches of the night,
no tears remain to wet my empty eyes.
You struck me so deep, so beyond healing,
that even in forgetting,
I am chained to remembrance.
Did you abandon me to these barren fields,
that your absence might carve your memory
deeper still?
Thanks, O thanks to you,
for the wound you gave without a word.
Thanks, O thanks to you,
for the ruin you wrought so silently.

I cast no blame upon your passing shadow
for it was my heart that opened the door.
Thanks, O thanks to you,
for leaving me forgotten beneath the wide,
indifferent sky.
Thanks, O thanks to you,
for the emptiness where once your name dwelled.

A Grave Beneath the Moonlight

The place where love resigns to die
is neither stone, nor hallowed ground
but sealed within the haunted hush
where once our spectral vows were found.
No dirge was sung, no petals wept,
just phantoms cast by argent flame.
Its grave was carved in sleepless thought,
a mausoleum forged from shame.
You wore your smile—a porcelain veil
unmoved by echoes torn apart.
But I, who cradled all your pulses,
now scavenge ruins of the heart.
I do not plead beneath the stars,
nor damn your name with bitter breath.
The moon—archivist of sorrow
has archived truths long past their death.
What's interred now was once my cosmos,
a love too proud to kneel or break.
And though I drift from what remains,
I trail a hush no dawn can wake.
Not all farewells are shaped by sound
some bloom like frost upon the ground.

Her Letters Burned

I cast her letters to the flame
each page a veil of perfumed lies.
Yet still the smoke, like mourning silk,
ascended through the twilight skies.
Though ink had faded, parchment thinned,
her phantoms stirred with every spark.
Each syllable a siren's wail,
each phrase a dagger in the dark.
She wrote of love in trembling gold,
of mornings steeped in seraph light.
But all her vows were half-conjured
the spells of one who fled the night.
The fire hissed with serpent tongues,
and cinders danced in cursed delight.
But pain, unburned, endured the blaze
for ghosts gain flesh in firelight.
Now silence wears her shadowed voice,
in tones too treacherous to trust.
The lines are ash, but I remain
a revenant of love and dust.
And all that lingers, lost yet live,
are lies that smoulder where I grieve.

The Elegy of Absence

You left no sound upon the floor,
no echo in the turning key.
You simply faded from the air,
like breath withdrawn from melody.
The walls still carry your gentle laugh,
the cup still bears your faded trace.
But I no longer find your eyes
in any corner of this space.
Your farewell was not a broken scream,
no curtain drawn in wrath or haste.
You left me flowers in the vase,
and took the fragrance, not the waste.
I waited for a letter, a word
some music whispered through the door.
But silence taught me all I feared:
you wouldn't come back anymore.
So, I walk the rooms with reverent steps,
not touching things that once were ours.
You were a dream too bright, too brief
a comet lost to other stars.
And though the hours will soften pain,
the empty room still knows your name.

The Thread Beneath the Floorboards

There was a thread, too fine to see,
that stitched your breath into my days.
It wound itself through casual words,
through glances passed in crowded ways.
I lived upon its quiet pull,
believing seams were strong and tight.
But now I walk on broken boards,
and nothing holds beneath the light.
The walls are still; the paint has dried;
your scent survives in empty drawers.
The books remain where you last placed them,
but I cannot read their lines anymore.
Was it a dream? Or just design
a structure made to fall in time?
The thread, I find, has come undone
and every step betrays the rhyme.
The house is hollow, filled with names
you never meant for me to find.
They speak in murmurs through the cracks
and pull apart the trusting mind.

Yet still I wander through these rooms,
searching for the place you tied the knot
a thread that once held love intact,
and now holds everything it's not.

The Hesitant Heart

Once, beneath a broken sky,
I wandered through the dust of dreams
Where silent clouds and withered winds
Bore witness to my severed seams.
My tears had turned to voiceless stone,
My steps had lost their living tone;
In the hollow chambers of my chest,
The song of life had come to rest.
The days fell past like autumn leaves,
The nights wove shrouds my soul could grieve.
Alone, I stitched the rags of pain,
And taught my hands to build again.
The bitter wine of sorrow drained,
And from the ashes, strength remained.
Yet even then, I dared not call
For love to rise within my wall.
But lo! One evening, soft and mild,
A stranger's gaze, a tender smile
As though the wounded sky above
Remembered how to speak of love.
She came as quiet rivers glide,
A hush upon the burning tide.

And in her voice, a twilight song,
That mended places broken long.
Yet still, my heart, a trembling bird,
Recoiled from even the gentlest word;
Afraid to trust the hand outstretched,
Afraid to dream, afraid to fetch
The shattered stars from ancient skies
Afraid once more to hope or rise.
O timid heart! Shall I not dare?
When morning's gold renews the air?
When even ruined gardens bloom,
And sorrow yields its thorn to plume?
Thus, faltering, I take her hand,
As twilight softens all the land.
And though the past still shadows me,
I choose, at last, to set it free.

When You Let Go

You held my hand in silent hours,
when even words were shy to speak.
You looked into my soul so deep
I thought you'd stay, both bold and meek.
Your breath was warm along my path,
your shadow danced beside my feet.
I trusted love to last beyond
the dusk where parting souls might meet.
But soft was the slip of your hand from mine,
a leaf that fell with no sound made.
And in that fall, the world grew still
all bloom undone, all colour fade.
Now I walk where memory hums,
and your echo lives in falling rain.
The skies still carry the shape of you
but never quite the same again.
You let go not with rage or cry,
but with a hush I could not fight.
And now my heart, though brave by day,
still breaks in shadows every night.
O love, you vanished with such grace,
you left not scars—just empty space.

The Last Lantern

I held your name—a flame in twilight's breath,
a trembling light the tempests could not quell.
It dwelt within my soul's secluded shrine,
a lamp of longing none could dare dispel.
You spoke as though from realms the stars have known,
your eyes—a firmament where silence sang.
And in the stillness woven through your voice,
I planted dreams where sacred echoes rang.
But love is fashioned out of vapor's thread,
and trust takes root in soil the winds betray.
One evening fell—you slipped beyond the veil,
and night unfurled in full, untampered grey.
The lantern sways beside the ashen door,
its glow—a vigil no one comes to tend.
It was not meant to light the path beyond,
but burn for vows too delicate to mend.
Now wind moves through the space where you once breathed,
and even dawns seem muted in their hue.

The flame endures—a frail, defiant star,
not kindled now by hope, but what is true.
No curse I speak, no tears my silence names—
yet still it burns, fiercer than sorrow claims.

The Last Meeting

It was the day we were torn apart forever,
And the wound of that parting will fade — never.
The sun hid itself behind a grieving cloud,
While the dusty wind roamed, wailing aloud.
My eyes, as if by fate, were fixed on you
And in that gaze, a thousand silent sorrows grew.
Our unspoken tears flowed, trembling and slow,
Witnesses of a love too deep to show.
After two long years of hollow silence,
You asked to take a photograph — our last remembrance.
You wished to bury it, quietly, somewhere unseen,
In the hidden corner where old dreams lean.
I could read your silent plea through your breaking eyes,
As we made a vow — without words, without lies
To hold this moment as long as breath remains,
Yet never to meet again, for fear of deeper pains.
And thus, we parted, each carrying a storm within,
While the dust and the sorrow swallowed the wind.

CHAPTER: 2
The Healing

When I Was Depressed

When I was depressed, the world grew still,
As though the earth had lost its will,
No lark did sing, no stream did glide,
The stars turned cold, the sun would hide.
I walked alone where shadows fell,
Within the silence of my shell;
For hearts that break in treasoned trust
Lie long beneath forgetful dust.
She spoke of love in summer's bloom
A rose that withered far too soon.
Her eyes were oaths, her hands were lies,
She fled beneath September skies.
And I, a wreck of love once fair,
Sat tangled in the ghost of care,
While voices of the night would say:
"She's gone, and love has passed away."
Yet time, the balm of bitter fate,
Unwinds the cords of wrath and hate.
I found a lake where lilies sleep,
And let my soul in silence weep.
I let the wind unclench my brow,
And learned to live, though not know how.

A quiet life of dawns and tea,
And books beneath the alder tree.
No crowds, no cries, no endless race,
But morning dew and twilight grace.
The scars she left still faintly gleam,
Like twilight's ghost in waking dream;
Yet peace—sweet peace, though slow to start
Has grown to shield my tender heart.
Though once betrayed, though once oppressed,
I am no more that soul depressed.
Through soft retreat and tranquil ways,
I walk unshaken all my days.
Let falsehood fall, let old wounds rest
I seek no more, for I am blest.

The Weight of Waiting

Who are you waiting for, my dreaming heart?
What promise holds you when it falls apart?
The road is still, and silence walks beside,
While time moves on with neither guilt nor guide.
No shadow walks these roads with me,
No arms remain where arms should be.
No soul will weep for you or mine,
No bonds remain, not even lies,
Why drown, dear heart, in breathless sighs?
No one shall die with us—none love so endlessly.
No hand shall share this borrowed ache,
No soul our shattered peace shall make.
Why grieve for those who never meant to stay
Who turned their backs and simply walked away?
You have no kin, and I no name,
Then why recall what never came?
Why rise this grief behind your eye,
When all has left, and none asks why?
Don't let your eyes keep searching through the rain
Not everyone is worth the weight of pain.
Let silence be the answer you embrace
Not all wounds scream—some heal with quiet grace.

Again, whose path do you await, O dreaming heart, alone?
The silence stretches miles, the years are carved in stone.
The world forgot you long ago
And me as well, this much I know—
Then why these tears you have never shown?

Let the World Whisper Still

Let them whisper — for whispering is their way,
The world will speak, though it has naught to say.
Why lose the night to fleeting, foolish sound,
When silence holds the stars more tightly bound?
This world has laws that twist and turn with time,
Each sunrise fades, unblessed by reason or rhyme.
Who are you — and what's a name worth here,
When Sita bore her fire, yet shame drew near?
Must every eye that gazes wide and wild
Drown your grace, as though truth stood defiled?
They call me lost in colours of delight,
As if love's bloom was born to hide from light.
But I have seen those very lips that scorn
Walk twilight lanes with secrets they adorn.
The ones who judge with hands so quick to stain
Have knelt unseen before desire's domain.
Did Radha not wait, heart split like a song,
For Krishna's flute that vanished for too long?
And Meera, drunk on love the world called mad
She danced through taunts, yet never once grew sad.
They bled in silence, mocked by mortal law,
But touched the feet of truth the world won't draw.

So let them talk — their words are dust and wind,
And we, who love, need not be caged or pinned.
Their fiction cracks when faced with what is real
For wounds may burn, but deeper wounds can heal.
So, tell me now, beneath this honest sky:
Who sins more—those who love, or those who lie?

Where Memory Let Go

How long must memory carry you,
Through corridors of thought?
I walked within your shining world
And never knew the cost.
Your voice, a chord of twilight bells,
Your look, a tide's command
It pulled me past the reach of self,
Into a distant land.
For years I lived beneath your light,
Entranced by what I knew;
But time, the quiet, wiser friend,
Revealed a deeper truth.
No final word fell from your lips,
No gentle parting line
Only the rain, in falling notes,
Spoke of what we left behind.
I searched the stars to hear your song,
A sign to hold on to,
But silence, like a deeper breath,
Told me what love could do:
That even shattered hearts can mend,
And still remain sincere

And from the ashes of a dream
A gentler strength appear.
Your voice once ruled my sleeping hours,
But now it fades with night;
For morning comes with softer steps,
And brings a kinder light.
So let the past be what it was
A chapter, vast and true;
Not bitterly cast to the wind,
But kept with love for you.
The road ahead is mine to walk,
Beneath an open sky
The sun has touched my face again,
And now, I will not hide.

Ashes of Departure

Let me rise
not from grandeur, nor from grace,
but from the hushed corners of loss
where names vanish, and memory
is a room with no furniture.
I have sat where silence leans,
have traced the cracked tiles of my heart
with fingers stained in echoes.
Let me breathe
not with the breath of lovers,
but with the solitude of trees.
She
she has the privilege of turning her head
onto borrowed shoulders,
each one dressed in tailored promises.
I, the pauper of affection,
have only the bend of my own spine
to weep upon.
Still, I rise.
Yes, I am poor
not in coin,
but in the luxury of consolation.

Yet, what is love that fails
but the opening of another sky?
What is sorrow but a language
we are all doomed to speak
before we learn silence?
You, who dance between velvet arms
rich in touch, poor in depth
know this:
there is a kind of wealth in ruin
when ruin does not beg.
I have walked past the alleys of grief,
fed crows my bitterness
and watched them ascend.
I have poured my longing into cracked vessels,
not to drink,
but to see the light seep through.
In the tremble of the streetlamp
and the hush of my own hands,
I learned:
to break is not to die
it is to melt.
You measure your worth in who remains;
I measure mine in what I become.
The world did not end in her eyes,
only narrowed.
And I have found horizon in the smallest things:

a rain-soaked bench,
an unopened letter,
a name that no longer cuts.
So let me be.
Let me rise
not into applause,
but into quiet.
Not to be loved again,
but to be.

An Hour Without a Name

The month withdrew, not dark, but dimly dressed
Its light like breath upon a mirror's chest.
The wind arrived in silken undertones,
And every lane recalled its stepping stones.
You left — not loud, but like a final thought
That slips between the silence we forgot.
I did not call — I only watched the day
Undo its seams and fold itself away.
The clouds, once sworn to travel side by side,
Drew separate maps across the evening tide.
So too, your name unstitched itself from mine
Not cruelly done, but as the stars decline.
I tried to hold — but how can hands retain
What's shaped from mist, and tethered not by name?
The will to keep was not a written part
Of love's curriculum, nor sorrow's art.
This city — unnamed, though pressed into my chest
Spoke not in words, but ash, wind, and rest.
Its lamplit hush, its benches lined with grey,
Bore witness when I let you walk away.
No echo stayed at the threshold's seam,
No vagrant leaf restored the vanished dream.

But still I stood where we had learned to be,
And touched the bark of our forsaken tree.
It's nature's law — the rivers cleave the land,
The petals fall despite the softest hand.
And birds, though once attuned to nesting two,
Will take to separate skies when dusk is due.
So be it — let the hour lose its name.
Let parting own no enemy, no flame.
The wind is not unkind for moving on,
Nor night to blame for shouldering the dawn.
And if I live — and live I surely shall
It will not be through bitterness, but fall:
The quiet fall of things that could not stay,
Yet taught the soul to meet another day.
So, mark this truth — no triumph, no regret
I walk where frost and fallen time have met.
And in that silence, I sometimes whisper a line
Not of what's lost, but what was once divine.

The Shadow of Farewell

I do not weep — the tears have left my cheek;
The soul may fracture, but the eyes stay bleak.
I do not seek you — neither in thought nor
in dream,
Commands my heart to drift along that stream.
Some pulse persists, beneath the practiced art,
Of turning silence into shield and chart.
The wound remains, but slowly, it is sealed
A mark now known, not hidden or concealed.
I do not wait — no voice commands me to stay,
No echo draws me back to yesterday.
Yet here I stand, though once I turned away,
Led by the steps my memory still obeys.
If I am seen through glass that time has blurred,
Then let it hold the shape of kinder words.
The heavens grieve with me — the rain descends,
Not as a storm, but as the ghost of friends.
The walls recall no voices now, but mine,
Each echo met with dusk, austere, divine.
By the alcove rests the ceremonial line,
The corded relic — obsolete, benign
No footfall sounds, no laughter strikes the air,

Yet stillness breathes a gentler kind of care.
I dwell where absence teaches how to breathe,
And plant what grief once taught me to unsheathe.
This house, though quiet, is no longer cursed
Its silence speaks, and not in pain, but verse.

The Day After She Left

The hour she left, the clocks refused their ticking
Time, suddenly disowned, hung limp in mid-air.
I tasted her silence like rust on my tongue,
And breath became an act I had to remember.
She did not depart with thunder,
But with the hush that follows a requiem.
No doors slammed. No curtain call.
Just absence entering like a learned guest
Uninvited, but already seated.
I rose with the morning and felt displaced,
As though I had borrowed my own body.
The light outside tried painting redemption,
But inside me — only blurred frescoes of her face.
Is this how memory matures?
Not into clarity, but into echo?
Each hour tolling the bell of what never returns.
I walked among relics
Her coffee spoon, her brush, a letter half-torn
And wondered if objects mourn more deeply
than men.
In my chest, a chapel built from bruised devotion,
Candles lit by habit, prayers unsigned.

Was love ever here, or only the need for it?
The soul, it seems, does not bleed all at once.
It oozes slowly, with sophisticated grief
A kind that wears spectacles, speaks in metaphors,
And sips solitude as if it were wine.
The day after she left,
I did not die.
That is how eternity begins
Not with angels,
But with surviving what should have ended you.

What the Evening Forgot

The air in your city moves different,
not colder, but kinder
as if even the breeze knew
not to disturb your hair.
Evenings settle like silk there,
folding themselves over the roofs
where shadows smoke from chimneys
and lamps flicker like hesitant promises.
I walked those lanes once
with your laughter folded into my coat sleeves.
Now, it's only the dust that speaks to me,
and the dry branches that remember
how you once paused beneath them.
And what of the heart?
Once, it was a cathedral
now only the echo remains,
moaning through ruined arches
where your voice used to sing.
I bore the sin of belief
believed you constant,
believed the stars we named together
would not burn out so easily.

But silence took root
where your hand used to rest.
And you
once the hymn in my throat
have become the ache
I recite alone.
How strangely sharp is the love
that turns its face away
not with fury,
but with the indifference
of someone who no longer checks
if you made it home safe.
Yet, here I remain
an older version of myself,
restitched by quiet mornings
and the discipline of forgetting.
There is a dignity in survival
no poem can rightly praise.
No orchestra plays
for the man who learns to eat alone
without mourning the silence.
I have gathered my shadows
and folded them neatly,
stored them in places
where grief can no longer enter.
And though you come still

sometimes in dreams,
sometimes in the steam
of a stranger's teal do not flinch.
You were the fire.
I was the paper.
Now, I am the ash and ash
no longer burns.

And Still, I Rise Alone

(after the leaving, after the asking)

O God—if You're listening, I won't ask again
Where You live or why You hid when I bled.
I've made peace with the silence You sent me,
With the prayers that came back undelivered.
Once, I curled like smoke around her memory,
Clung to the scent of what couldn't stay.
I mistook pain for proof,
And waiting for love.
But now I wake.
Not whole, not loud—but awake.
Like first light cracking through shut windows,
Like breath that finally stops apologising.
She left, yes.
And it shattered the song I'd built us.
But I've learned
Even broken things echo if you speak to them kindly.
No more tracing the sky for her return,
No more begging God for answers
To questions that were meant to break,
Not to solve.
Because faith isn't always about finding

Sometimes it's about walking anyway,
Even when the map has burned.
Frost was right: the road does diverge.
And I have chosen mine
Not the one that leads back to her,
But the one that leads back to me.
Let the nights come. Let the old ache stir.
Let her name pass like wind over water
Soft, gone, never owned.
I am not a ruin.
I am the voice that rose from rubble.
I am not waiting anymore.
O God, if You're anywhere
Be in the steps I take today.
Forward. Unshaken. Free.

The Body Remembers What the Mind Denies

She left—yet her absence walks through my chest,
Not as thought, but as weight: a tired kind of breath.
I don't speak of her anymore
But my spine arches when someone says stay.
Grief has its own geography.
It settles in muscles, folds into sleep,
Twitches beneath smiles I've taught myself to wear.
The mind—so clever—redacts, revises, forgives.
But the body?
It holds the truth like an old wound pressed into a book.
There are mornings I wake as a ghost in my ribs,
My heartbeat unsure if it should trust the sun.
Even laughter feels borrowed, like a coat not mine.
I have survived her—but survival is not peace.
She is gone.
But her name still echoes down my nerves
Not as memory,
But as instinct.
Healing does not come like spring.

It comes like winter learning to breathe again.
And this skin
It remembers not the love,
But the leaving.

The Destiny That Waited in Silence

I knelt where endings come to pray
Beneath a sky unstitched from mercy,
Where silence rang more sacred than bells,
And love—once fire—had turned to scriptless ash.
She left, and time unclothed me.
Not in wrath, but revelation,
She vanished like a verse withdrawn by God
Not erased, but never meant
To reach its final line with me.
Even the stars had rearranged their witness.
Grief was not an ache, but a rite
An initiation into the hidden order
Where sorrow is a veil for truth,
And loss the first gesture of the divine
Before it speaks in flame.
I wandered, yes, through dusk-stained thought,
Through cathedrals hollowed by her name.
But I saw, in the dust of despair,
That fate is not stitched by mortal longing
It is inscribed where we do not see.
She was not promised—only permitted,
A brief lantern held in shadowed hands.

And when she fell from the thread of my days,
I did not fall
I was redirected.
The Unseen has a finer ink,
A scripture written on the silence between days.
What breaks us sometimes builds the altar
What leaves us opens the gate.
And so, I rose—diminished, yes, but destined still.
For somewhere, beyond the reach of my ruin,
Another voice was being carved for me,
In temples where I had not yet prayed.
And the path un-walked, once feared,
Now bore the quiet scent of my becoming.
I stepped forward—not to forget,
But to fulfil.
The ashes cooled. The breath returned.
And destiny, once veiled in sorrow,
Began its deeper vow.

Not the Ache, but the Awareness

At midnight, when even sorrow lay in silence,
I turned to the Gita*—not as commandment, but as companion.*
Its verses did not thunder. They breathed
soft as the hush before dawn,
and waited, like Krishna beneath the peepal tree
still, until my soul leaned in.
"Be not the ache," it murmured,
"but the awareness that beholds it."
My hands—still scented with goodbye
folded not in penance,
but in the fragile shape of forgiveness.
Arjuna's unrest echoed my own
a heart too gentle for the battlefield of absence,
yet too alive to retreat.
And like him, I knelt not in defeat,
but in a longing to understand
what love asks of the broken.
Krishna spoke, not of conquest,
but of compassion stitched into courage.
He spoke of karma—not as burden,
but as the art of offering

each deed like a rose at the feet of the Eternal.
I closed the book
with the war still breathing in my chest
but this time, my hands held the reins
like a prayer fulfilled in motion.
And there, between silence and scripture,
I found peace—not in escape,
but in the quiet nobility of surrender.
Not the surrender of falling
but the rising,
when one finally trusts the divine timing.
In that sacred silence ,
the Gita *became my own heart speaking:*
Live. Love. Let go.
And lift again—softly, certainly , like the stunning morning.

The Cartography of My Unmaking

(a hymn to the earth that held me when I broke)

I did not send postcards
for what is a place but a silence in motion?
But the hills—ah, the hills—wrote epistles in my marrow,
scribed in wind and lichen,
a grammar of forgetting I had not yet learned.
The rivers absolved me before I confessed.
They pulled my name through braided silt,
where memory grew moss-soft, and less cruel.
Each eddy became a psalm,
not of loss, but of relinquishment.
Banaras received me without inquiry,
like a mother who reads dreams on her child's skin.
The ghats asked nothing
they only gave me stone wide enough to vanish upon,
and time enough for vanishing to feel like grace.
Himachal whispered: rise above it.
At nine thousand feet, sorrow loses weight.
The air is thinner where names can't cling
and grief, untethered, becomes only mist.
In Ujjain, beneath the pendulum breath of Mahakaal,

I stood still enough to feel eternity pulse through ruin.
Some endings are spoken in reverse
I mistook them once for goodbyes.
The Sundarbans, tangled in fanged roots
and twilight,
taught me that beauty need not beg for softness.
Survival itself can be sacred.
Sri Lanka—where the sea bleeds stories
offered no mercy, only mirror.
But there, I bowed to the tide,
and it did not drown me—it named me pilgrim.
Kolkata, beloved in its disorder,
held me like a lullaby sung in a forgotten tongue
some cities don't ask for your best,
they remember your original voice.
Cherrapunji rained not water but renewal
Each drop spoke like monks in moss-hung cloisters,
and I wept for how gentle it felt to be undone.
In Uttarakhand, I met silence
so vast, it had echoes of God in it.
Faith there wore stone—not scripture
and stood with the dignity of unmoved time.
Even the Thar, austere in its loneliness,
did not pity me.
It gave me the sun like a compass,
and shadow as a place to rest.

I no longer chased her silhouette
through the alleys of memory
I sought instead the kind of light
that does not remind, but reassembles.
These places did not mend me
they refused to name my sorrow.
They simply let me stand as if I had never fallen,
and breathe—like one who remembers
they were always whole.

The Return That Was Never a Journey

I climbed to peaks where clouds wore saffron robes,
Thinking thin air might hush the echo of her
But dawn, that old betrayer, spoke her name
In light that kissed the pines like old devotion.
The mist, more loyal than memory itself,
Carried her silence with monastic grace,
A ghost now fluent in the breath of sky.
In Banaras, where time walks barefoot, slow,
I watched the Ganga take my whispered griefs
As if my prayers were hymns she once had sung,
And every diya drifting down the tide
Was her retreat, rehearsed a thousand ways.
Even fire bore her posture of farewell.
I sought the sea, imagining erasure.
But salt remembered what the mind would drown;
Each wave returned the weight I once cast off
Grief, like driftwood, always floats back home.
No shore could hold what soul must carry still.
Healing, I learned, is not a place, but penance.
In temples carved from inner hush, I knelt.
Mantras passed through me like wind through a flute.

Still, she remained—less woman now, more wind
A myth I met in every breathless chant.
I wandered cafés with a borrowed tongue,
Where strangers poured their solitude in cups.
Yet in the clink, a laugh that wasn't hers
Still shaped her shadow in the steam and sound.
Then I unfastened every map I'd made
Let milestones dissolve into metaphor,
Let roads turn back like rivers to their spring.
I tired of running from a flame gone cold,
And let the ground beneath me bear my weight.
Somewhere beyond the compass of desire,
Between the ache of "still" and grace of "gone,"
I found a kind of home within my name
Not hers, not ours, but mine, long overdue.
The world had not forgotten me, I learned.
It only waited till I could return.

Unlearning Her Gently

I had carved her name into the temple of my breath
not with desire, but devotion.
Now, I must erase her, not in grief,
but in the same silence
with which monks extinguish the evening lamp.
My palms still tremble with her farewell
they fold unconsciously,
as if her absence were a hymn
they had once been taught to recite by heart.
I no longer tread the road where she dissolved
yet the dust remembers me,
clinging like soft ash to bare feet,
like questions left at the altar
when gods do not answer.
At twilight, she returns—not as herself
but in the lilt of wind-chimes,
in strangers whose voices
carry the warmth of her yesterdays.
But I let them pass,
like Ganga lets go of lotus petals
never meant to return upstream.
Grief had made its shrine inside me

with incense of what-ifs
and walls of longing.
But I have begun the quiet ritual of undoing:
brick by softened brick,
I sing it down with newer songs.
Healing is not the exile of memory,
nor the conquest of desire
It is the sacred art
of loving what was
without needing it to remain.

The War Was Mine

The day dimmed not as light withdraws,
but as a prayer abandoned mid-thought
its flame not extinguished,
but paused in the silence between longing and letting go.
Twilight, amber-clad and unassuming,
bent over my shoulder like a mother who knows
the child is too tired to ask for answers.
I reached not for God—no,
I had no hymns left in me.
What I sought was sanction
a benediction not to rise,
but simply, to continue.
I opened the Gita, *not as disciple,*
but as one undone by devotion.
And Krishna
he did not summon tempests
nor stir the sky into moral thunder.
He spoke—quiet as breath inside a broken chest.
He said,
"You are not the ache.
You are the one who watches it ache."

I did not argue.
Grief had made me fluent in silence.
And in that moment, I saw
not her, but the memory of her
as Vapour lifting from a cup long emptied.
It rose.
It did not return.
The Kurukshetra of my being
was never in the world beyond
it throbbed beneath my ribs,
a conflict not of nations,
but of narratives.
The war?
It was between who I had been in her eyes
and who I must now become
without them.
That night
I did not cast her out from memory.
I merely ceased to kneel before it.
I folded the book not in conquest,
but in quiet comprehension.
And I knew
some stories are not healed.
They are outgrown.
And I, still breathing,
was proof.

When I No Longer Spoke to Her Memory

One morning, the ache forgot to arrive.
No tremble in the tea,
no sigh caught in the scarf she once touched.
Her voice no longer echoed
in the corridors of thought.
Even nostalgia—my most faithful thief
came empty-handed.
I did not bury her;
I outgrew the need to resurrect.
There was no thunderclap,
no choir of angels
only the quiet clarity of absence
replaced by presence.
The soul, once tethered to a grave of glances,
now wandered
not away, but within.
Even my shadow no longer shaped her outline.
The birds still sang their meaningless songs.
But I hummed with them.
The poem I once wrote in her name
began, at last,
to rhyme with mine.

Where I No Longer Seek Her

I no longer seek her name in the wind's old tongue,
nor tether my worth to the relics of farewell.
The ache, once etched into the bones of dusk,
now sleeps—dimmed like embers post
incantation.
I crossed the deserts sewn with her vanishing,
where silence did not echo but endured
not as absence, but as vow withheld in breath.
Even the stars, once thorns in memory's crown,
have gentled into softer constellations.
Not every twilight must resemble her sigh.
Let it be known—the monsoon came not
to drown,
but to teach the soil the syntax of forgiveness.
And I—no longer bent beneath her leaving
stood, not as the forsaken,
but as the one who stayed and dared to remain.
My scars no longer clamour for spectators.
My voice no longer mimics her vanishing.
I've cloaked myself in the saffron of solitude,
and in its holy hush, I found my name—unbroken.
Love was never the wound, but the water
not a blade, but a river—severe, sculpting.

It carved my grief into cathedral bone,
and from its tide, I rose—not shattered,
but shaped.
Not ruined, but re-written in the language of bloom.

What the Mirror Forgot to Say

Each dawn I stood before that spectral pane
a brittle oracle of glass and ghost,
where silence hung like judgment in the light,
and truth was trimmed to outlines at the most.
It traced the arch of jaw, the sunken eyes,
but missed the wars still folded in my chest;
no tremor of the breath was rendered there,
no echoes of the nights I'd not confessed.
It did not dare to speak the sacred phrase:
"You were brave to remain when all had fled."
It did not lift its voice to softly say:
"You, the forsaken, still rise from the dead."
What glass can hold the weight of unseen scars?
What light reflects the ache that hides from stars?
Yet silence stood, as silence often does,
where pain wears robes too fine for mirrors' gaze.
No hymn, no thunder, no immortal verse
just breath, and bones, and unrecorded days.
And so, one morning, calm with earned unrest,
I placed my palm upon that breathless frost
not seeking flaws, nor vain pursuit of form,
but to forgive the man the glass had lost.

The one who bore the ghost she left behind,
who gathered self where no applause was due,
who learned that healing wears no laurel crown,
but walks in shadow, slow and tried and true.
I turned—not out of shame, nor weary grace
but to behold the soul the glass erased.

The Morning After Her Shadow

The kettle sang — not of longing, but of light,
its steam a slender psalm rising from sleep's ashes.
No ghost laid claim to the threshold of thought,
nor did her scent haunt the hollows of dawn.
Daylight arrived without apology,
unfastened from the scent of her leaving.
It draped my shoulders like a shawl once mine
not gifted, not stolen—just mine, at last.
The mirror, once an accomplice in ache,
reflected me whole—not fractured by memory.
Not a trace of her name in the hollows of breath,
not a whisper of grief curled on the rim of the cup.
The birds outside rehearsed no parables.
They sang not to remind, but to be.
And I, no longer prisoner to recollection,
let their song pass through me like wind through a veil.
I did not dig through the marrow of yesterdays
nor ransom joy for the price of remembrance.
The tea, though lukewarm, tasted of now
not of lips once kissed, but of lips still mine.
A line from the Gita *swam softly ashore:*
"He mourns not who knows the truth of being."

This time, I received it without resistance
as one receives rain when parched but not pleading.
Even the silence in the room felt unburdened
not empty, but wide, like the sky reborn.
Even divinity, once distant, drew close
not in temple tones, but in the breath between.
No smile lit my mouth, nor song my tongue,
yet peace sat beside me, quiet as flame.
And I breathed—not to recall, not to forget
but to begin, in the full majesty of now.

The Letter I Never Sent Her

I once wrote to you
not with pen, nor on paper,
but in the silence between heartbeats,
where breath turns brittle with remembering.
Each word was a tremor I dared not hold,
inked in nerve and the ache of restraint.
The silence between us—vast, unspoken
roared louder than any parting ever dared.
I began with your name,
but it unravelled into mine too quickly.
Strange, how grief alters grammar
how every sentence bends
like a spine that's prayed too long for return.
I wanted to say:
I forgive you.
But my hands faltered,
as if writing those words
might call your absence back again.
You see, love did not die
it fossilised.
And I am learning how to live
with a museum inside my chest,

each memory under glass,
untouched, yet aching.
I remembered the time
you laughed until tears spilled
and I didn't yet know
those tears were rehearsals
for how we'd end.
This was never a letter
only a letting go.
A folded sorrow
tucked between the pages
of a book you never finished.
I never sent it
because healing needs no address.
Only a moment
when you finally choose yourself
over the echo of someone who never stayed.

Where the River Did Not Ask

I came to the river with her name on my tongue,
a syllable trembling at the edge of surrender.
But the current, indifferent, did not ask
it moved like truth: unsoften, undented.
Beneath me, stones older than sorrow
lay unbothered by my ritual ache,
offering no gospel,
only the sermon of having endured.
I sat with my grief like a stunned bird
its wings folded into the memory of flight,
bones hollow with things unsaid.
The water sang—not of hope,
but of letting go with dignity.
No shrine awaited.
No priest lit incense for absence.
Not even her shadow haunted the reeds.
Yet I was seen
seen by something vast enough
to witness without asking why.
That evening, I did not heal.
But I unclenched the name
I had wielded like a blade

against my own remembering.
I set it down.
Let it drift.
Not buried
but returned.
The river did not hold it.
And so, I began to un-hold too.

Where the City Left Me

I came to her like myth comes to flame
seeking warmth, or at least, a direction.
But her lungs were borrowed from smoke and neon,
and her nights wore perfume
to veil old bruises.
I believed healing might rise
on station platforms thick with departure,
in the silence where coffee curls
around someone else's laughter.
I wandered her aisles of forgotten books
as if dog-eared truths
could mend the syntax of my sorrow.
I traced my name on fogged glass
to ask the moment if I still remained.
The roads turned their backs,
the river kept her distance.
Even the sanctuaries
silent, solemn
held no echo of my ache.
Only pigeons, winging like unsent psalms,
brushed the bleached noon air.
The city did not save me.

Yet she withheld ruin.
Instead, she taught me
healing is not some garlanded hour
outside the self.
It arrives unceremoniously,
like verdicts do
in the loneliest chamber,
where you must sit beside your hunger
and learn the grace of feeding it.
I left the city with no answers.
But the silence I carried
was no longer borrowed.
It was mine.

What the Mirror Forgot to Say

Each dawn I stood before that spectral pane
a brittle oracle of glass and ghost,
where silence hung like judgment in the light,
and truth was trimmed to outlines at the most.
It traced the arch of jaw, the sunken eyes,
but missed the wars still folded in my chest;
no tremor of the breath was rendered there,
no echoes of the nights I'd not confessed.
It did not dare to speak the sacred phrase:
"You were brave to remain when all had fled."
It did not lift its voice to softly say:
"You, the forsaken, still rise from the dead."
What glass can hold the weight of unseen scars?
What light reflects the ache that hides from stars?
Yet silence stood, as silence often does,
where pain wears robes too fine for mirrors' gaze.
No hymn, no thunder, no immortal verse
just breath, and bones, and unrecorded days.
And so, one morning, calm with earned unrest,
I placed my palm upon that breathless frost
not seeking flaws, nor vain pursuit of form,
but to forgive the man the glass had lost.

The one who bore the ghost she left behind,
who gathered self where no applause was due,
who learned that healing wears no laurel crown,
but walks in shadow, slow and tried and true.
I turned—not out of shame, nor weary grace
but to behold the soul the glass erased.

The Bloom After Rain

A resurrection in thirty-three lines

It did not come in splendour, nor in flame
no trumpet sorrow, no valiant fall.
It came like dusk between two prayers
subtle, almost embarrassed to arrive.
The ache crept in like ivy on old stone,
naming me before I knew I was lost.
I shattered in unlit corners of speech,
where silence drips like a slow betrayal.
Not in laments, but in half-dreams,
in the pause after her shadow faded.
The world wore noise. I wore the silence.
No psalm fit the quiet of my undoing.
Healing began not with angels or dawn
but with wet earth clinging to my soles,
a worm writhing where roses once slept,
the taste of ash in morning's first tea.
I dwelled in wreckage, not waiting for light
but listening to its absence hum like truth.
One day, a heron crossed my sky of thought.
A leaf kissed my shoulder without warning.
I did not recoil.

The Ganga murmured beneath Manikarnika,
not of endings—but of recurrence.
Even my grief bowed to that rhythm.
I wandered through Himachal's breathth
in air teaching me how to stay.
With the Gita *curled like a secret in my coat,*
I stood before the void and did not kneel.
I uttered no forgiveness. I was forgiveness.
And the sky—hollow, vast, unapologetic
became kin.
Now, I water the soil inside my chest
without fearing the stormy cloud's return.
The petals I grow do not pray for mercy.
They bloom knowing they may drown
and still, they bloom.
This is no echo of pain.
This is the hymn after fire,
the soft defiance of a soul re-rooted.
If you must name it,
call it what it became
The bloom after rain.

Chapter 3: Finding Love Again

A Study in Her Delight

She is not one who enters
rather, the air adjusts itself to her imminence.
The walls recede, light falters at her hem,
and even the geometry of silence
bends in deferential pause.
Her speech is no mere utterance
It distils,
like incantations left unsaid
between the creases of forgotten psalms.
It lands like snow
not cold, but too immaculate to touch
without trembling.
Each gesture dismantles logic
not symmetry, not style,
but the sacred entropy of grace.
A spoon held still.
The crook of an elbow.
The inarticulate theology
of her looking away.
Her laughter
no eruption, no aria
but a fugitive sound,

like candlewax whispering
its surrender to flame.
Ephemeral,
but heavier than thunder once it's gone.
She is not tempestuous
and yet not ever tame.
She is the tremor beneath restraint,
a sonnet losing form
at the scent of skin.
The echo that answers
before you know the question.
Her delight is a studied unravelling
not merriment,
but a discipline of deferral:
the fruit un-plucked,
the syllable suspended,
the fire withheld
by choice, not fear.
Even her ire arrives lacquered in restraint,
like a verdict spoken
through silk and unwept sleep.
A chastisement so tender,
it begs to be mistaken
for a plea.
She does not disturb the world—
she recalibrates it,

with the back of a knuckle,
and suddenly
it remembers
how to listen.
She is no mortal citation
she is the space between epics,
the punctuation of longing,
the soft gravity
that makes collapse seem beautiful.
No orchestration
just a lone cello,
tuning itself
beneath the breath of the divine.

What My Eyes Have Chosen

A letter, not of longing, but of arrival

Ask me
Were I to enter a hall steeped in splendour,
where every object gleamed with the weight of my former desires,
where voices I once admired hung in the air
like incense,
and every face bore the calm authority of the known
what would I search for
And I would say:
nothing.
For I have been stripped of the old hungers.
Once, I too believed love was the finding.
Now I know — love is what unmakes the search.
In crowds
dense, humming with the noise of need and name,
beneath lights that expose but do not reveal
my vision holds still.
I do not scan. I do not falter.
I remember.
And my memory

wears the shape of your gaze.
You are not one among the beautiful.
You are the exile of categories.
The exception that undoes the rule.
The still point in a storm of symbols.
And when I behold you
not as body,
but as the only silence my eyes can rest within
then all the world's arrangements
shatter into irrelevance.
What need have I
for stars, for names, for mirrors?
Your presence
renders the architecture of desire redundant.
You are not the goal of my searching
you are the end of search itself.
And yet
even the soul that has arrived
must walk.
Even love,
when known, must be re-earned
with the ache of re-seeing.
So let me wander,
not away from you
but around you.
Let me carve through the noise of cities,

through rooms too loud with beauty,
through voices begging to be believed
only to return to that which never needed proving.
For in the cathedral of a thousand eyes,
mine shall remain undistracted.
Not because you are loud,
but because you are true.
And the true does not shout
it draws.
What my eyes have chosen
was never a choice.
It was the oldest vow
etched in a language the heart remembers
when the world forgets.
So, if you ask me again what I would seek
I would say:
I seek nothing.
I simply walk the distance
between knowing and remembering you.

The Imperfect Geometry of Love

For you remain my dream-drenched sleep,
Where silence holds what I cannot keep
The hush of noons, the still of night,
The soft rebellion of fading light.
For you, I shelter mischief eyes,
Where laughter flickers, then softly dies.
And in the vaults of mind's retreat,
A love lies folded—raw, discrete.
You need not be, my dear, refined,
As Einstein's proofs, exact, aligned.
No symmetry must stitch your name
Be rather my mistake in flame.
Be the forgotten line I meant
To write in ink but dreamed in scent
A flaw I loved too much to mend,
A wrong that shaped the perfect end.
You need not swell like sky's expanse,
With godlike calm or starry stance.
Be rather my moon—abrupt, unsure,
That hangs above my ache, obscure.
The moon that burns in blistered noon,
A quiet grace, a clumsy boon

That breaks the sun with borrowed light,
And calls me home from out the night.
Let them seek heavens vast and pure,
I'll keep the heart that's less secure.
For even flaws, in love confessed,
Are holy ruins—made and blessed.

Upon Seeing Her Once

I saw her,
Not in dream, nor in dusk,
But in the lucid cruelty of day,
Where nothing hides and beauty rarely lingers.
Yet there she sat, as if the hour had knelt to her
A Bengali girl in woven grace,
Her sari folding time in pleats of gold and dusk,
Eyes rimmed in kajal like twin eclipses,
Not dark—but divine.
Her gaze—O God, her gaze
A quiet deity stood there,
Not sculpted in temple stone
But breathing through her lashes.
The room became a shrine,
And I, unworthy of worship.
A ukulele in her lap,
Its strings sighed beneath her fingers
Notes trembled like first rain on a prayer bell.
Her voice, no louder than a thread in air,
Yet every vowel carried the weight of monsoon and moonlight.
She was not speaking

The divine was borrowing her throat.
Her playfulness—what the poets would call nakhra
Was no less than the poise of a crowned girl
Twirling anklets in a mirror of fate.
She asked for nothing
And yet the world bent slightly toward her,
Like trees bowing to a passing breeze,
Unaware of their devotion.
There are beauties born for the eye
Then there are those made for silence,
For the ache in the poet's hand,
For metaphors that kneel unfinished.
I could write her forever
And never begin.

Where Your Shadow Falls

What would you truly know, my love,
Of how this heart—once quiet as morning dew
Now thrums like a veena strung by longing's hand,
Each note trembling for the echo of you?
You walk untouched by the ache you cause
A sovereign of silence, dressed in dusk.
And still, I breathe as if the air were yours,
As if your absence were a fragrance I must trust.
This heart speaks not in whispers, no
It dreams aloud in the chambers of the unseen.
Had you lingered just a moment longer,
Time itself might have folded in between.
You
You are the moment before rain meets earth,
The silence before the temple bell is rung.
I, the beggar beneath your windowpane,
Left to hum verses never sung.
You made a pilgrim of this drifting heart,
A seeker bound to a star not charted.
Tell me, then, is guilt mine to carry,
When it was your gaze that first started
The fire beneath these careful bones

A glance that scorched, then turned away
Yet left behind a shrine of echoes
Where memory kneels every day?
O woman with eyes like ancient seas,
So endless I forget to breathe
If names hold power, as the poets claim,
Then tell me softly: what do you believe?
And though I now remain a mere silhouette,
Lost in the haze of your untold hours
Let me not lament what life withheld
Let me find worship in the quiet of your powers.
If I shall not hold your hand in this unfolding
Then let me carry your unspoken dreams in mine.
Let me walk beside your shadow at dusk,
And name it love, for all of time.

The Touch of Love

Ah, what was this life I once led,
A mere shadow of purpose,
A drifting leaf on an endless stream
An existence devoid of worth.
The world, so bright in its allure,
Veiled within, a tempest of sorrow,
I knew not when it veered and swirled,
But soon, my days became nothing but a snare,
My every step, a restless echo in the void.
Time, once a faithful companion,
Now slipped through my fingers like sand,
My heart scattered in a thousand places,
Lost in a labyrinth of disquieted thoughts.
I fell into the deep well of despair,
Where the silence weighed heavy on my soul,
And yet, amidst the darkened storm,
A gentle rain descended
A balm, a whisper from the heavens.
In that moment, the earth itself seemed to sigh,
As if it reached out to cradle me,
And for the first time, I touched
The essence of love.

Now, I know
The love I sought was never far,
It was you, my beloved, standing eternal,
A guiding star in the vast night of my existence.
The time I once squandered in aimless wandering,
Now passes with purpose, swift as a river's course,
Your smile, a beacon, illuminates my dreams,
And in your gaze, I have learned
Life is not merely a fleeting journey,
It is a deep well of meaning,
And though the road be harsh and fraught with strife,
In its very struggle lies
The touch of love.

In the Hues of My Soul

You are painted in the hues of my soul,
Who are you, my dearest, my heart's silent call?
Are you the vision that haunts my dreams,
The elusive pause in the endless streams of time?
Are you the love that stirs this beating heart,
The ache unspoken, tearing me apart?
I falter, unable to voice
The depths that lie in me, so drowned in choice.
Yet still, I feel
Between us, something unspoken, something real, has healed.
When I close my eyes,
Your smile remains, a beacon in the night's disguise.
When you sit beside me,
Heaven touches earth, a grace so pure, so free.
Is this what they call love, this trembling sigh?
I cannot hold it, nor fully comprehend why,
But one thing is certain
I love you, and only you, beneath the endless sky.

The Silence I Wear Like Skin

I cannot name this love.
No phrasing fits its quiet weight.
It does not shout; it does not shine
It lingers like a half-closed gate.
I do not trace it in the stars,
Nor map it out in measured time.
It is a breath that holds its shape,
A hush that rhymes beneath all rhyme.
When someone else's eyes find you
My soul folds in, but does not show.
The heart convicts, yet signs no name;
It burns too deep, too slow.
You'll never know the things I tame
How many storms I stitch in sleep.
I let you go, a hundred times,
And each return is mine to keep.
That day, the wind touched your shoulder,
And something in me bent to pray.
You never knew—your eyes looked on
But all of me was given away.
There's worship in the things unsaid:
The way your shadow spills through doors.

You walked ahead—I walked behind,
Like rain that wants no more.
They say the ache of absence fades,
But they have not been left by you.
The clocks still move, the world pretends,
Yet nothing old feels new.
Each day without you leans, not breaks
But still it leans, and so do I.
And every hour finds its edge
Somewhere beneath your sky.
This isn't longing—it's becoming:
A quiet law I can't suspend.
You live beneath my breathing now,
Where distance has no end.
So, ask me not how far love reaches.
It is the ache I wear like skin.
You were the door I stepped inside
And now I live within.

The Silent Love

My mind lost its wandering way,
The moment, I beheld you that first day!
The first shy smile upon your lips
Drew my gaze into fathomless depths.
The fragrance of your loosened hair
Melted my senses into the evening air.
The longer I gazed, the farther I flew,
Not knowing where my lost thoughts drew.
Through the gentleness of your tender care,
My broken heart found a hidden repair.
Yet I knew not when time, with silent tread,
Betrayed my dreams and left them dead.
You linger still behind my dreaming eyes
A silent love, breathing in unseen sighs.

Symphony of Breath

A symphony breathed through the stillness of life,
A rhythm borne of the heart's own strife
You are the Gitanjali, my visions recite,
A dream-song woven in silken light.
Through corridors carved in the soul's embrace,
You blossom like jasmine—timeless in grace,
A fragrance that lingers on memory's skin,
Soft as dusk fall, yet fierce within.
Whether the road is fleeting or wide,
Through silent woods or the city's tide,
Your thought returns—a sudden tide,
And I, though surrounded, feel denied.
Among the many, I search in vain,
Your absence echoes in each refrain
A solitude cloaked in a thousand eyes,
Where silence, not speech, underlies.
Yes, like monsoon rain on sacred wood,
Like thunder's dance where calm once stood
Our love defies both wound and delight,
It lives beyond the veil of night.
We are fated to rise through time's deep art,
To meet once more, heart after heart

Not once, but through a thousand births,
To claim again what love is worth.
This love—so tender, so vast, so true,
Breathes beyond all that time can undo.
It waits in the hush between dusk and dawn,
In the soul's own rhythm—drawn and withdrawn.
To gaze into you, to call your name,
We shall return through life's old flame.
Again and again, through time's own hand,
I'll find you there—where stars still stand.

An Earnest Wish to Meet You

There dwells within my soul a quiet plea
To meet you once, and part from you no more;
To lose myself within your eyes, and see
Reflections only we were meant to store.
To wait by your side as hours unfold,
With fingers laced, through evenings flushed with gold.
To wander gently where the stillness grows,
And let the silence between us softly close.
A yearning stirs—to smooth your tresses down,
To watch your laughter, chase away a frown.
To craft a life where we, in tender grace,
Might journey time as one, in one shared place.
To stand with you through anguish and through song,
To lift your grief, and hold your joy lifelong.
To never bear the ache of drawn goodbyes,
But dwell with you where true belonging lies.
To call you mine in voice and soul and name,
To rest within your arms, unashamed, the same.
A vow—to gift you all my light and peace,
And from your sorrows grant your heart release.

To carve my days around your sacred worth,
And be the fire that warms your quiet earth.
This is my wish—enduring, vast, and true:
To meet, and live, and love this life with you.

A Quiet Flame

She walks as if the wind has learned her name,
Each step a whisper, delicate and slow
Like petals falling, soft without a claim,
She moves through silence, setting hearts aglow.
Her grace is not the kind that asks to stay,
But lingers, like a secret shared in trust;
You breathe her in—and something drifts away,
Some fear, some weight, some grief reduced to dust.
She speaks—and every edge of pain turns round,
Her voice, that sings without a sound.
It curls like smoke around the shattered heart,
And every word, a stitching of the part
That broke before she ever knew your name
And now, somehow, you're never quite the same.
Her touch—God help me, how do words compete?
It's not a touch, but light that wears a skin.
It finds the part of you that feels defeat,
Then warms it, dares it to begin again.
A single brush against my furrowed brow,
And all the noise of life grows soft, grows slow.
I feel like rain that's kissed a thirsty tree
Alive, and home, and everything I'd be.

She smells of lilacs, rain, and something more
A memory that's never touched the floor.
It clings to shirts, to songs, to passing days,
It dances in the dark like candle blaze.
I catch it once, and all the world stands still,
As if the wind itself obeys her will.
Her eyes—don't ask me how to speak of those.
They're not just eyes; they're doors that never close.
They don't just see—you fall through them instead,
You lose yourself, and find your soul has bled.
But not from pain—from love so deep, so wide,
You drown with joy, and dream with arms
flung wide.
They're galaxies that open when you stare,
And somehow, you forget the world was there.
So don't you say that beauty's just a phase
Not when she lights the dark with steady blaze.
She blooms in ways that time can't touch or steal,
A rose that dares the frost to feel.
She is the calm beneath my loudest fight,
The reason I believe that wrongs turn right.
And I, once broken, now stand up again
Because she taught me love is born through pain.

Am I Truly Worthy?

Am I deemed worthy, efficient, O dear?
The dream I've cherished, lucid and clear,
Is locked within the mirth of your smile,
A joy that lingers, a blissful while.
The stars above, the winds that sing,
And the golden sun's soft whispered fling,
All seem to ask, in silence profound
Am I deserving of your love unbound?
When you smile, the heavens draw near,
A fleeting vision of paradise, pure and sincere.
I cannot fathom what love truly means,
But without you, life feels but barren scenes.
Yet, your eyes, they ask with a haunting gaze
Am I worthy of your love, in all my ways?
Am I efficient, in your gentle sight,
To hold your heart through day and night?
O fleeting moment, where doubt takes
its reign,
Asking myself if I am pure, or stained,
Am I enough to make you see,
That your love is all I yearn to be?

Your elegance, beyond words, too rare
to describe,
A purity that leaves all questions aside.
All they seem to ask, in silence, aglow
Am I enough, for your heart to know?

The Road of Love's Embrace

The road ahead, serene and vast,
Stretched gently 'neath a sky enshrouded,
A silence deep, where time held fast,
Awaiting a whisper, softly clouded.
The hum of the bike, my sole refrain,
As the cool breeze grazed my face,
While rain, like secrets, fell in vain,
Anointing the air with sacred grace.
And then, as though the heavens had willed,
Your arms embraced me, warm and near,
The solitude of the path was stilled,
Dissolving in the radiance of you, my dear.
Your voice, as soft as twilight's sigh,
Spoke words that lingered in the fading light:
"I love you," you announced, from your heart's pure core,
And the world blossomed, bathed in light.
In that instant, nature stood as witness,
To a truth profound, untouched by years
No dazzling light, nor tempest's fitness,
But a vow that transcended all fears.

How could I forget those words, so true,
A love that knew no bounds of space or time?
In that embrace, I knew with you,
The boundless road was ours to climb

The Things I'll Never Forget

How could I ever forget what your eyes once said
A glance that sang what lips could never thread?
No need for sound when silence bore your voice,
In that one gaze, you left me with no choice.
I saw a world where I was not alone
Just you, and time, and moments overgrown.
You walked beside me—streets turned soft and slow,
The world grew quiet just to let us go.
Each heartbeat timed itself to match your pace,
As if the hours bent to grant us grace.
We laughed in ways that echoed through the air,
Like childhood dreams too perfect not to share.
Your scent—still caught in folds of afternoon,
Like flowers breathing under silver moon.
It rises in the air when I recall
Your hair cascading like a gentle fall.
I breathe, and there—you're standing close again,
A memory wrapped in jasmine, silk, and rain.

The moment you would enter, light would shift
The room would pause, as if you brought the gift
Of dawn itself—the shadows bowed in awe,

And every soul forgot what else they saw.
Even the sun, in reverence, lost its flame,
As if the skies knelt softly at your name.
Your hand in mine—that miracle, that peace
All questions stilled, all aching found release.
No need to speak—our silence knew the way,
Where fingers touched, our hearts would always stay.
You were the road, the journey, and the end,
A thousand lifetimes folded in a friend.
So, ask me not to leave these days behind
They're stitched into the corners of my mind.
Where time runs fast and seasons learn to bend,
You are the moment I would always send
To every storm, to every tired breath
A name I'll carry past the doors of death.

When I Speak of You, My Love

When I speak of you, the winds hush mid-flight
Not for meaning,
but for the memory my breath still carries of
your name.
It is not spoken—it arrives,
like a whispered hymn in a ruined cathedral
of thought.
Your name is the softest invocation I've ever known,
a syllable so sacred, even silence dares not interrupt.
You walk not in steps, but in cadences
the kind only old souls recognise.
You are the poem I have feared to write
too luminous for language,
too eternal to be sealed in ink.
Each time you move, the earth forgets its orbit.
And I, this foolish disciple of your being,
chisel psalms into my hours,
as if God loaned me clay just to shape your grace.
Your eyes—they are not mere sight.
They are ancient portals where entire lifetimes kneel.
Shrines, where even my deepest prayers
seem like borrowed echoes.

When you blink, constellations alter course,
and myths rewrite themselves to match your
quiet mystery.
Your silence is not absence
It is the divine breath before creation itself.
And your laugh—ah, your laughrings like temple bells
shivering through monsoon mist,
a sound I would tattoo into time,
if time would stay still long enough to let me.
I would never pamper you with gold
It tarnishes too easily.
But my gaze?
It would wrap around your soul like incense
around deity.
Each morning, I'd wake you not with alarms,
but with affirmations spun from reverence:
"You are exquisite, even in your unguarded hours."
"Even when your dreams cling to the corners
of your eyes."
I'd oil your hair like tending to sacred vines
growing in temples left to memory.
I'd kiss your forehead like tracing sacred geometry,
not out of obligation
but because loving you feels like kneeling
at the altar of something far greater than flesh
You would never need mirrors while I breathe .

my voice will mirror back the fire you forgot
you carried.
Because you, my love,
were never just a woman.
You are composed of centuries,
of collapsed galaxies,
and of prayers unspoken by men who never dared
to ask the stars anything more.
But if you ever vanish from this realm
if time dares to steal you into its unkind fold
know this:
I will raise my voice only once,
to call your name across centuries
so loud that even forgotten gods remember us.
And if fate tears you from this life,
my poetry will haunt the next.
For your beauty was never meant to perish
It is the poetry my soul was born to recite
until the end of all remembering.

She, Who Returns Me to Myself

There are mornings carved in alabaster
where the light moves like memory,
halting, reverent,
as if reluctant to disturb
what is already divine.
She is such a morning.
Not an epiphany that shouts across skies,
but a recollection
as if my soul had known her once
in a life too ancient for time to recall,
and now, at last,
the forgetting ends.
She is not flamboyant like ecstasy,
but precise
like the final stroke on a master's canvas
that makes all chaos coherent.
Her silence does not fill space
it defines it.
I have walked through years
that felt like abandoned stations,
where no train ever comes,
and conversations begin only to collapse.

But she
she enters like the rarest white spring morning,
soft as truth,
clean as absolution.
She is the hush
between thunder and rainfall
not the spectacle,
but the secret.
And I, a weary tenant of noise,
learn to listen again.
Her presence is a cascade of stillness,
like a waterfall
falling not to break
but to polish
every jagged part of me.
She is sleep to a pilgrim of wakefulness
not escape, but return.
No more borrowed beds,
no more ceilings that question belonging.
In her breath,
my name finally makes sense.
She does not announce herself in metaphor.
She is the metaphor.
And even the dew,
that polite ambassador of dawn,
bows before her gait.

She is not a muse;
she is the manuscript.
Not inspiration,
but incarnation.
Her lips do not utter love
they recite it.
With the kind of fluency
that renders all poets irrelevant.
Where others disrupt time,
she arranges it
folds the days into sonnets,
and threads my chaos
into the symmetry of a single gaze.
She is not the fire that devours
she is the hearth.
And in her quiet light,
my most unruly shadows learn to sit still.
She is the only geography
where I do not need direction,
only arrival.
And in her,
I arrive.

When the Gaze Undoes Time

There is a manuscript behind your gaze
unspoken, yet aching to be read.
A scripture of love inked
not in letters,
but in the tremble of eyelashes
and the hush that follows your breath.
Let me read it, just once.
Not as a boy who rhymes
to impress the moon,
but as a man who has known silence
and wishes now to sing again.
I have worn the robes of restraint,
walked alone through the corridors of reason,
but your eyes
they disobey time.
They draw me back to the fever
I once locked in a drawer of poems
never sent.
Once, I longed to be Byron
storming through sorrow,
but you...
you make me wish to be Eliot,

piecing fragments of devotion
into something whole.
Your presence is not a metaphor
it is the verse itself.
Your face, a leather-bound book
that smells of old ink and
something holy.
Your smile,
a footnote to every prayer
I never knew I was whispering.
When you speak
not in declarations,
but in the accidental poetry of everyday
your lips release lines
that put all my verses to shame.
I do not envy the poets before me.
I pity them
for never having known you.
If ever your voice
were to shape itself around my name,
even once,
I believe the stars would rearrange.
I do not seek possession.
I seek presence.
Let me be woven
between the folds of your day,

subtle as a bookmark pressed
between chapters you never rush.
Love, in your eyes, is not a fire
it is a quiet inheritance.
And I
Only ask to inherit a line.
Let me read.
That is all.
I do not wish to conquer the world.
I only wish to be a sentence
in the book
you open when no one else is watching.

The Name that Lives Inside

What else within this heart may lie,
But you, the breath of morning sky?
No whisper hides, no shadows stay
You are the pulse that guides my day.
And if this heart were opened wide,
Your name would shine from every side
Not etched in sorrow, not in pain,
But gilded like a golden rain.
I'd heard of love from lips of lore,
But never knew its truth before
Until your voice, so soft, so clear,
Made all the world grow bright and near.
My dreams were stars adrift and free,
Until they found their home in me
Through you, whose grace and light appear
In every breath, in every year.
No restless fire, no aching flame,
Just joy that gently spoke your name.
Your presence like the hush of night,
Turns every shadow into light.
They speak of heaven's realms above,
But I have found my heaven — love

Within your eyes, a boundless gleam,
More vivid than the boldest dream.
You walk beside me, calm and near,
Your voice the song I always hear.
My soul, once scattered, now is whole
You are the compass of my soul.
There's nothing more I seek to find,
With you, the world is kind, aligned.
My heart, a sacred space for two
Each beat a prayer that sings of you.
So, tell me, love, what more could lie,
Within this heart, beneath this sky?
There's nothing left to glorify
But you, whose love will never die.

What the Moon Whispered to the Sea

Her presence did not arrive like light
it came like remembrance.
Soft as the breath between two silences,
and full of all the truths
the heart speaks only when alone.
It is not beauty that defines her,
but how her nearness reshapes stillness
how rooms forget to echo when she enters,
how even time
lingers a little longer
in her wake.
She is not present to be seen
she is felt,
like warmth in a place
where winter has always lived.
As though some ancient ache
found rest simply by sharing space with her.
I have watched oceans hush themselves
beneath the gentleness of her being;
the moon, once austere,
bends low

in quiet reverence.
Not because she asks
but because the world remembers how to feel
in her presence.
Stars recalibrate their distance
not to impress her,
but to remain near enough
to witness her stillness bloom.
Her presence does not demand
it restores.
It tells me—without gesture or word
that grace may still enter a tired life,
unannounced,
like rain over a ruined field.
And I
I am merely the soul who once stood beside her,
and was changed,
not by what she said,
but by who she allowed herself to be
fully, quietly,
and eternally.

Even Himachal Remembered "Her"

I wandered where the ridgelines sleep
beneath their robes of snow—
through Himachal's silence, where breath
becomes a visible prayer.
The sky
a pale silence stretched across pine needles,
hung with the weight of yesterday's snow.
A fog rose gently,
like incense offered to some forgotten god,
and the sun
a cautious eye
blinked once through the veil of rain.
It was beautiful.
But not enough.
Because somewhere between the hush of trees
and the brittle glint of frost on stone,
you arrived
not in form,
but in memory
and with you came
that blush of a smile
I never truly held.

That smile
God, it was not carved for mortal air.
It did not belong to valleys or to storms.
It was the pause in winter
when snow falls slower,
ashamed to touch the earth.
Even the mountains,
with their white-tipped arrogance,
stood humbled in your name.
I watched a ray of sun
thread its fingers through clouds,
and thought
not even that light could touch the world
as gently
as your lips did
when they turned toward joy.
The pines wore snow
like ageing poets wear grief
with grace, with stillness.
But your smile wore silence
like a secret just born
soft, unsure, and holy.
And what could this land offer
to rival that?
What is mist,
if not the way your breath

once trembled in laughter?
What is the hush before snowfall,
if not the stillness I felt
when you looked at me
with nothing said
and everything meant?
I came here seeking quiet.
But Himachal spoke your name
in every rustle,
every thaw,
every surrender of rain to light.
Even the fog,
I think,
was trying to shape itself
into your smile.

More Than a Face in Varanasi Light

She moves not for the gaze, but for the grace,
Like Ganga's breath that gilds Kashi's face.
Her soul flows pure—serene, unstrained, and wide,
A sacred silence beneath the fervent tide.
Not for the jewels she may choose to wear,
But for the joy she casts upon the air.
She is, to me, what Ganga is to Varanasi
Not scenery, but spirit; not fleeting, but steady.
She walks like verses written in old stone,
Through alleys where the dusk has softly grown.
In lanes of Varanasi, where time forgets to weep,
Her essence dwells, in silences that sleep.
As sweet as Malaiyo at break of day,
That melts upon the tongue, then drifts away
So light, so rare, so born of breath and dew
Her laughter lingers just as softly, too.
Her eyes—still pools where Ganga's aarti gleams,
As if the stars had slipped into her dreams.
Her voice—refined, like temple bells at rest,
A silence composed where sanctity is blessed.

Her nature—like Kashi's twilight repose:
Mature, eternal, fragrant as the rose.
She is no moment's flame, no fleeting fame
But the sacred quiet that love dares not name.

Where You Are Touched by My Colour

Where you are touched by my colour's hue,
I wonder—are you dream or true?
A muse who stepped from myth and mist,
Or simply love, in human kissed?
You walk as though the world must pause
As if your breath rewrites its laws.
And in your gaze, too vast to name,
I see the spark before the flame.
Are you the story stars once wrote
Across the sky in silver note?
Or just a girl who dares to stand
Inside the circle of my hand?
Tell me—why does the starlight burn
Each time your eyes begin to turn?
Why does the wind, just grazing you,
Bring fragrance where it never knew?
And why, tonight, does silence swell,
As if the world forgot its shell?
Why does the night lose all its grace
When shadows gather near your face?
You seem unsure, though softly bright,

A figure formed of flame and fright.
Your voice is quiet—yet I hear
The trembling of a distant year.
Your scarf slips slowly from your side,
As if your soul no more can hide.
And in my chest, a subtle storm
Takes shape within your shifting form.
We stand as though we've just begun
Two hearts undone, yet strangely one.
No vows are said, no promises,
But something deeper presses this.
We are, perhaps, not meant to speak.
The truth between us runs too deep.
It hangs in air, it floods the ground,
It makes no noise, yet shakes all sound.
So, tell me now, or let me know
By silence, smile, or evening's glow.
If I am dusk and you are dawn,
Then why must we remain withdrawn?
Where you are touched by my colour's hue,
I see the world reshaped by you.
Not fairy tale, nor ghosted line
But something mortal, warm, & divine.

When You Came Near

Since you came near, the noise withdrew.
The world, once frantic, found its hush
My heart, a city lit by longing,
Felt the lamps dim and quietly burn for you.
I no longer solve for unknown destiny;
There is no logic in missing someone.
What joy could any answer give
When your absence is the only unsolved proof?
You changed my inner landscape
No cartographer could draw this ache.
Without permission, you shifted the stars,
And I, who once walked straight,
Now drift toward you with every thought.
I stopped praying to gods for my needs,
Now I bow to the silence
Just before your message arrives.
This is not rebellion,
This is reverence.
They think I sneak out in defiance
But I leave in search of something sacred.
I lie, not to deceive,
But to preserve the only truth I know: you.

You ask what love has done to me.
It has bruised me gently,
Taught me how to ache without bleeding.
It has turned a boy into a man
Who trembles at the thought
Of losing something real.
Your love is no light thing.
It is weight—glorious, holy weight
Pressing into the ribs
Like a name carved deep.
Let them promise you stars.
I offer you silence.
The kind that holds you when no one else stays.
And if your father is the last gate
I will not beg.
I will knock, steady, once.
And let my love speak
In the language of constancy.

When I Stood Before Her Silence

I stood before her silence—not the kind
That simply waits, but one that holds the wind.
Her eyes, two lanterns swung from distant time,
Lit thoughts I hadn't dared to make into rhyme.
No throne of gold, nor heavenly design,
Could shape the stillness of her breath like mine.
She wore the dusk as if it knew her name,
And every breeze around her came in flame.
O love—if beauties ever walked this place,
She did, in quiet—with no need for grace.
Her voice was not the sound of choral flight,
But rain that speaks to thirsty earth at night.
I did not speak at first. My soul had knelt
Long hours in shadows where her nearness dwelt.
The trees around us bowed with listening leaves,
And even time grew hesitant to breathe.
What words could hold her name and not fall short?
What promise built in mortal tongue or court
Could match the way her silence touched my chest
As if my restless heart was put to rest?
I said
"If all the stars should lose their glow,

And winter bury every rose in snow
Still, I would come to find you in the frost,
For what is pain, when you're the cost?"
Her lashes lowered, slow as drifting cloud.
The world, for once, forgot to be so loud.
And in that hush, I found the ancient truth:
That love does not arrive—it waits, uncouth.
I told her
"You are not made of flesh and flame alone.
You are the silence between the wind and stone.
You are the reason that the owls still call,
And trees keep waiting for the leaves to fall."
If she had wept, the sky might well have wept.
But no—she held her breath, and silence crept
Like some divine decision, still and sure
The kind no priest, nor poet, could endure.
And so, I said, with voice not loud, but clear:
"If love must live, then let it live right here.
I do not ask for kingdoms, stars, or vows
Just the soft right to call your silence ours."

Where Your Embrace Begins

If I should beg, when nightfall sighs,
To rest beneath your tender skies,
Would you, with lips of silken flame,
Still kiss my fears and speak my name?
If laughter blooms upon my face
Because your love adorns my days,
Will you, though shadows drift and bend,
Refuse to leave, or let it end?
The evening stole the sun's last gold,
Yet still you linger, soft and cold.
You turn away, your silence pressed
My heart remains your lone confessed.
Will you, with grace in every thread,
Let falling fabric, finely spread,
And eyes adorned in charcoal shade,
Undo the vows my soul has made?
I live because I dare believe
That in your arms I shall not grieve.
Without your breath, this world turns pale
A ship unmoored, a song gone stale.
And if I fall to dreamless sleep,
Where none return, and none may weep,

Then find me in that hush divine
Where dreams and love in stars align.
I hold you close within my chest,
Where thoughts undressed have come to rest;
Each whispered ache, each hidden plea
I gather them and set them free
You turn to silence, bruised with pride,
But still I stand, with arms flung wide.
I speak of sorrow, soft, contrite
And lose the war to your delight.
For even wrath becomes a grace
When mirrored in your quiet face.
I wear my frown like winter's frost
Yet one small smile, and all is lost.
I live because I dare believe
That even time you will outlive.
And should I sleep that final night,
Then come and hold me past the light.

She Walks My Heaven Barefoot

She moves as morning spills upon the grass,
Unknowing of the light her presence lends;
No rule she keeps, no need for gloss or glass,
Yet every glance, a silence the daylight sends.
Her laughter breaks like birds from trembling trees
So sudden, pure, it makes the stillness dance;
And I, who bore the weight of centuries,
Now live and breathe within her sweet mischance.
She forgets the time, the thread, the name,
Yet in that storm of soft unknowing ways,
She builds a temple out of common flame
A home where even silence softly stays.
Her hair, uncombed, in dusky rivers falls
And I, the priest of such a sacred mess,
Unravel strands like prayer from temple walls,
To find in each loose curl her loveliness.
She wore a sari just for me one night
With childlike pride she turned, her cheeks aglow;
And in her joy, I touched the edge of light,
And felt the world grow quiet, full, and slow.

What king could dream of such a rich delight?
No crown could match the smile she gave to me.
For in her gaze, I knew my long, hard fight
Had won not gold—but love's simplicity — very divine!

The Girl of a Thousand Storms

She frets at clouds I cannot see nor feel,
A flick of wind and tides in her heart reel.
The teacup shakes, her brows begin to storm,
O Love! Her rage—so small, yet wildly warm.
She pouts, retreats to silences so wide,
I chase her ghosts, to stand by her soft side.
A single breath I steal, she turns away,
As if my love had cost her light of day.
But oh, she weeps if she has caused me pain,
Her pride dissolves like dew beneath the rain.
Though always right (in truth, she oft is not),
She lays her thorns where I had placed my thought.
She holds her fears like stars clutched to her chest,
Worries of wounds I've never once confessed.
She'd rage with fire if I forgot to eat,
Yet starve herself to make my hunger sweet.
She storms the room, a queen without her crown,
Then laughs so soft the angels all kneel down.
A thousand whims, a world inside her gaze
I'd lose my mind and thank the Lord for days.
Her love—a tempest robed in jasmine air,
She fights me fierce, then braids my name in prayer.

No logic binds her, nor does reason stake
She is the truth that dreams and madness make.
A paradox, a child of holy strife,
With every tantrum, breathes into my life.
She strikes me dumb, yet fills my tongue with song,
The fire and lullaby where I belong.
O let the bards of time confess and write,
That such a girl did walk beneath the night.
She broke the world in petals, thread by thread
And every ruin bloomed where her love bled.

About the Author

Dr. Sougat Dasgupta is an award-winning astrologer, poet, and spiritual thinker whose work bridges the ancient and the intimate. With years of experience in astrology, occult sciences, and healing through Vedic wisdom, Sougat has guided countless individuals across the world on their path to self-understanding and inner transformation.

His poetic voice was shaped not just by the books he read, but by the silences he survived. *The Bloom After Rain*—his debut collection—is the culmination of heartbreak, solitude, healing, and rediscovered love. Each poem bears the imprint of someone who has walked through fire, but chose to plant flowers in the ashes.

Sougat holds degrees in technical, literature and spiritual philosophy, and is certified in multiple astrological systems, including **Vedic Astrology, Vastu**, **Palmistry**, and **Mantra Therapy**. He is a Bioengineer, from National Institute Of Technology. Known for blending psychological insight with metaphysical tools, making his work both grounded and transformative.

Whether he's writing verses by the Ganga, interpreting a birth chart under the stars, or helping someone navigate the storms of life, Sougat believes in one truth above all: **healing is possible—and often, it begins with words.**